AI-POWERED PERSONALIZED STORYTELLING:

I0427525

DEVELOP AI ALGORITHMS THAT CRAFT PERSONALIZED AND EMOTIONALLY RESONANT BRAND STORIES BASED ON INDIVIDUAL CONSUMER PREFERENCES AND BEHAVIOR

BY

HENRY E. PARKINS

1

COPYRIGHT PAGE

TABLE OF CONTENTS

INTRODUCTION

In the ever evolving landscape of marketing, the art of storytelling has emerged as a powerful tool, capable of forging deep connections between brands and consumers. As we navigate through an era marked by unprecedented access to data and technology, the concept of personalized storytelling has taken center stage, transforming traditional marketing approaches. Welcome to "AI-Powered Personalized Storytelling: Develop AI algorithms that craft personalized and emotionally resonant brand stories based on individual consumer preferences and behavior."

Definition and Importance of Personalized Storytelling in Marketing

At the heart of this exploration lies the recognition that storytelling, when tailored to individual preferences, becomes an invaluable asset in the marketer's arsenal. Personalized storytelling transcends generic narratives, offering a bespoke experience that resonates on a personal level with consumers. By tailoring brand

10

stories to the unique tastes, interests, and values of individuals, businesses can elevate their marketing strategies from mere transactions to meaningful engagements. In this book, we delve into the essence of personalized storytelling, dissecting its definition and unveiling the profound impact it wields in the realm of modern marketing.

Overview of the Role of AI in Crafting Personalized Brand Stories

Enter the realm of artificial intelligence, a revolutionary force that is reshaping the way brands communicate with their audience. AI is not merely a technological marvel; it is the catalyst that propels personalized storytelling into new dimensions. Within these pages, we navigate the landscape of AI algorithms, understanding how machine learning, deep learning, and natural language processing collaborate to craft narratives that are not just personalized but dynamically responsive to individual nuances. This book serves as a guide for marketers seeking to harness the power of AI in storytelling, transcending the limitations of conventional approaches and embracing a future where brand communication is both intelligent and intimate.

Significance of Understanding Consumer Preferences and Behavior

Amidst the myriad of data points and digital footprints left by consumers, the understanding of their preferences and behaviors emerges as a cornerstone of effective storytelling. This book places a spotlight on the significance of delving deep into consumer insights, exploring the patterns that shape decision-making processes. By unraveling the mysteries of consumer behavior, businesses can create narratives that not only capture attention but also resonate emotionally. The ability to anticipate needs and tailor stories in alignment with individual preferences becomes a competitive advantage, and herein lies the essence of a strategic and impactful marketing approach.

Embark on a journey where storytelling meets technology, where AI algorithms become the architects of narratives that bridge the gap between brands and their audience. Join us in unraveling the intricacies of AI-Powered Personalized Storytelling, where innovation meets emotion, and marketing transforms into a personalized experience like never before.

CHAPTER 1

UNDERSTANDING CONSUMER BEHAVIOR

Analyzing Consumer Preferences

1. Importance of Data Collection and Analysis

In the intricate dance between consumers and brands, data stands as the silent maestro orchestrating the symphony of preferences. The significance of data collection and analysis cannot be overstated in the realm of personalized storytelling. In a world inundated with information, understanding what resonates with individual consumers requires a meticulous examination of their digital footprints, interactions, and choices.

This section explores the methodologies and technologies employed in the collection and analysis of consumer data. From the nuances of online behavior to the subtleties embedded in purchase histories, we uncover the wealth of insights waiting to be gleaned from the data landscape. The narrative unfolds in the exploration of data-driven personas, allowing marketers to peer into the minds of their audience and craft stories that not only align with preferences but also anticipate them.

2. Identifying Key Elements Influencing Preferences

Preferences are not arbitrary; they are the sum of myriad influences shaping an individual's choices. From cultural backgrounds to personal values, understanding the key elements influencing preferences is the key to unlocking the personalized storytelling potential. This section delves into the psychology behind consumer preferences, unraveling the intricate web of factors such as socio-economic status, lifestyle, and psychographics.

Through case studies and real-world examples, we explore how successful brands have identified and tapped into these key elements to create narratives that resonate with diverse audiences. By dissecting the anatomy of consumer preferences, we equip marketers with the knowledge needed to infuse authenticity and relevance into their storytelling endeavors.

Behavioral Patterns

1. Exploration of Common Consumer Behaviors:

Consumer behavior is a kaleidoscope of actions, reactions, and interactions. Unraveling the complexity of behaviors allows marketers to predict and respond with narratives that strike a chord. This section embarks on a journey through the varied landscapes of consumer behavior, from impulse buying to meticulous decision-making processes.

Through the lens of behavioral economics and cognitive psychology, we examine the triggers and motivators that propel consumers to act. By identifying common behavioral patterns, marketers gain a nuanced understanding of their audience's journey, paving the way for narratives that seamlessly integrate into the consumer's decision-making process.

2. Implications for Storytelling:

The synergy between behavioral patterns and storytelling is where the magic unfolds. This section bridges the gap between analysis and application, guiding marketers in translating insights into narratives that captivate and compel. By aligning storytelling strategies with the stages of consumer behavior, we uncover the art of crafting stories that are not just heard but embraced.

Explores the Methodologies and Technologies Employed In the Collection and Analysis of Consumer Data

In the realm of personalized storytelling, the collection and analysis of consumer data form the bedrock upon which the narrative architecture is built. This chapter delves into the intricate methodologies and cutting-edge technologies employed in the pursuit of understanding consumer behavior and preferences, guiding marketers toward a more profound connection with their audience.

Methodologies for Data Collection

Surveys and Questionnaires:

Traditional yet effective, surveys and questionnaires allow marketers to directly inquire about preferences, opinions, and experiences.

Utilizing digital platforms, these tools can gather a wealth of information, providing valuable qualitative insights.

Social Media Listening:

Harnessing the power of social media, marketers can analyze conversations, comments, and mentions to gauge public sentiment.

Real-time monitoring enables rapid response to emerging trends and consumer discussions.

Web Analytics:

Examining website traffic, click-through rates, and user interactions provides valuable insights into online behavior.

Tools like Google Analytics offer a comprehensive view of user journeys, helping marketers optimize content.

Purchase History Analysis:

Transactional data unveils the products and services consumers prefer, shedding light on their purchasing behavior.

Understanding patterns in purchase history aids in tailoring personalized recommendations and offers.

A/B Testing:

Marketers can experiment with different versions of content, products, or user experiences to observe how consumers respond.

A/B testing allows for data-driven optimization by identifying the most effective elements.

Technologies for Data Analysis

Machine Learning Algorithms:

Leveraging machine learning, marketers can predict consumer behavior based on historical data.

Algorithms can identify patterns, segment audiences, and recommend personalized content with increasing accuracy.

Natural Language Processing (NLP):

NLP enables the analysis of textual data, such as social media posts and customer reviews, to understand sentiment and extract meaningful insights.

Chatbots powered by NLP enhance customer interactions, gathering data in natural conversational tones.

Predictive Analytics:

Predictive models use historical data to forecast future trends, helping marketers anticipate consumer preferences.

These models inform strategic decision-making and enable proactive, rather than reactive, storytelling.

Customer Journey Mapping:

Technologies that visualize the customer journey help marketers understand touchpoints and interactions across various channels.

By mapping the customer journey, marketers can identify opportunities for personalized storytelling at each stage.

Big Data Analytics:

Big data technologies handle vast amounts of structured and unstructured data, extracting meaningful insights.

Advanced analytics on big data sets enable a holistic understanding of consumer behavior.

Ethical Considerations

Privacy Protection:

Striking a balance between data collection and consumer privacy is crucial. Marketers must prioritize transparent practices and adhere to data protection regulations.

Consent and Permission:

Obtaining explicit consent for data collection ensures ethical practices. Marketers should communicate the value of personalized experiences and respect consumer choices.

Data Security:

Implementing robust cybersecurity measures safeguards consumer data from breaches, instilling trust in the brand-consumer relationship.

As we navigate the methodologies and technologies of data collection and analysis, ethical considerations must remain at the forefront. The responsible use of consumer data not only builds trust but also sets the stage for the creation of truly impactful and emotionally resonant brand stories.

The Psychology behind Consumer Preferences, Unraveling the Intricate Web of Factors Such As Socio-Economic Status, Lifestyle, and Psychographics

Understanding the psychology behind consumer preferences is a nuanced journey through the intricate interplay of various factors that shape individual choices. In this exploration, we unravel the complex web of socio-economic status, lifestyle, and psychographics, offering marketers a deeper insight into the minds of their audience.

Socio-Economic Status (SES)

Income Level:

Psychological Impact: Income influences a consumer's perception of value, luxury, and affordability.

Implications for Preferences: Preferences may be shaped by a desire for exclusivity, budget constraints, or the pursuit of premium experiences.

Occupation and Education:

Psychological Impact: Occupation and education levels contribute to self-perception and aspirations.

Implications for Preferences: Consumers may be drawn to products and narratives that align with their professional identity or intellectual pursuits.

Social Class:

Psychological Impact: Social class influences lifestyle, attitudes, and values.

Implications for Preferences: Preferences may reflect a desire to signal social status, conform to societal norms, or seek differentiation.

Lifestyle:

Hobbies and Interests

Psychological Impact: Personal interests shape identity and contribute to a sense of fulfillment.

Implications for Preferences: Brands aligning with consumer hobbies can create emotional connections and resonate with their passions.

Cultural Influences

Psychological Impact: Cultural background molds values, aesthetics, and traditions.

Implications for Preferences: Understanding cultural nuances allows for the creation of culturally resonant narratives. Health and Wellness:

Psychological Impact: The pursuit of health and wellness reflects a consumer's commitment to self-care.

Implications for Preferences: Preferences may lean toward products and stories that promote well-being and a healthy lifestyle.

Psychographics

Personality Traits:

Psychological Impact: Individual personalities influence decision-making and lifestyle choices.

Implications for Preferences: Tailoring stories to match personality traits enhances relatability and emotional resonance.

Values and Beliefs

Psychological Impact: Core values and beliefs shape a consumer's moral compass.

Implications for Preferences: Brands that align with consumers' values create authentic connections and foster brand loyalty.

Attitudes and Opinions

Psychological Impact: Attitudes and opinions reflect a consumer's worldview and perspectives.

Implications for Preferences: Crafting stories that align with prevailing attitudes enhances relevance and engagement.

Implications for Storytelling

Personalization:

Recognizing the diverse psychological factors at play allows for the creation of personalized narratives that resonate with specific consumer segments.

Emotional Triggers:

Understanding the psychological underpinnings of preferences helps identify emotional triggers that can be leveraged for impactful storytelling.

Cultural Sensitivity:

27

Awareness of cultural influences ensures that brand stories are culturally sensitive, fostering inclusivity and avoiding inadvertent missteps.

Aspiration and Identity:

Crafting narratives that speak to consumers' aspirations and help shape their identities enhances the brand-consumer relationship.

In the realm of AI-powered personalized storytelling, the fusion of psychological insights with data-driven algorithms creates narratives that not only understand but also empathize with the diverse and intricate psychology of consumer preferences. This understanding serves as the bedrock for storytelling that transcends the transactional, fostering enduring connections between brands and their audience.

The Varied Landscapes of Consumer Behavior, From Impulse Buying To Meticulous Decision-Making Processes

Embarking on a journey through the varied landscapes of consumer behavior unveils a dynamic spectrum that ranges from spontaneous impulse buying to meticulous decision-making processes. This exploration not only sheds light on the diverse ways individuals navigate their purchasing choices but also guides marketers in tailoring narratives that resonate across this intricate spectrum.

Impulse Buying

Psychological Triggers:

Emotional Urgency: Impulse buying often stems from emotional triggers such as excitement, fear of missing out (FOMO), or immediate gratification.

Implications for Storytelling: Crafting narratives that evoke emotions and urgency can prompt spontaneous decisions.

Point of Sale Influence

In-Store Displays and Promotions: Physical cues and

promotions at the point of sale can trigger impulsive reactions.

Implications for Storytelling:
Narratives that emphasize limited-time offers or exclusive deals capitalize on the impulsive nature of these moments.

Social Validation

Peer Influence: Seeing others make quick purchases can create a sense of social validation.

Implications for Storytelling:
Stories that highlight social trends, popularity, or social proof can drive impulse buying behavior.

Meticulous Decision-Making Processes

Information Gathering:

Extensive Research: Consumers engaged in meticulous decision-making often conduct thorough research before making a purchase.

Implications for Storytelling: In-depth content, such as product guides, reviews, and expert opinions, aids consumers in their research process.

Comparative Analysis:

Feature and Price Comparison:

Meticulous decision-makers compare features, prices, and benefits before arriving at a conclusion.

Implications for Storytelling:

Narratives that transparently present product details and benefits contribute to informed decision-making.

Brand Trust and Loyalty

Building Trust over Time:

Meticulous consumers value trust and often stick to brands they perceive as reliable.

Implications for Storytelling: Consistent and authentic storytelling builds trust, contributing to long-term brand loyalty.

Bridging the Gap with Storytelling:

Narratives for Impulse Buyers:

Compelling Visuals and Urgency: Short, visually impactful stories with a sense of urgency cater to impulse buyers.

Personalized Recommendations: AI-driven algorithms can analyze past behaviors to provide personalized recommendations that align with impulsive tendencies.

Narratives for Meticulous Decision-Makers

In-Depth Product Stories: Long-form content, such as detailed product stories and case studies, appeals to meticulous decision-makers.

Educational Content: Providing educational content within narratives helps consumers feel empowered to make informed choices.

Unified Brand Story

Consistency across Journeys: Regardless of the consumer's approach,

maintaining a consistent brand narrative ensures coherence and reinforces brand identity.

Adaptive Storytelling: Dynamic storytelling that adapts to different consumer behaviors ensures a seamless and engaging experience.

AI's Role in Personalized Storytelling

Behavior Prediction:

Analyzing Past Behavior: AI algorithms can analyze past consumer behavior to predict future tendencies, assisting in tailoring stories accordingly.

Real-Time Adaptation: AI enables real-time adjustments to storytelling based on ongoing consumer interactions and behaviors.

Personalized Recommendations

Data-Driven Suggestions: AI algorithms utilize consumer data to provide personalized product recommendations and content suggestions.

Anticipating Needs: Predictive analytics within AI assists in anticipating consumer needs, aligning with both impulse-driven and meticulous decision-making journeys.

CHAPTER 2

THE POWER OF AI IN PERSONALIZED STORYTELLING

Introduction to AI Algorithms

1. Machine Learning and Deep Learning in Storytelling:

In the intricate dance between technology and creativity, machine learning (ML) and deep learning emerge as the maestros, orchestrating a symphony of personalized narratives. Machine learning algorithms, with their ability to analyze vast datasets and identify patterns, serve as the backbone of AI-powered storytelling. Deep learning, an advanced subset of ML, enables the exploration of complex relationships within data, allowing for a more nuanced understanding of individual preferences.

As we delve into the realm of AI algorithms, we uncover how these technologies decipher the intricacies of

35

consumer behavior, learning from past interactions to predict future preferences. The narrative unfolds with the exploration of real-world applications, showcasing how machine learning and deep learning algorithms become the storytellers, adapting and evolving with each consumer's journey.

2. Role of Natural Language Processing (NLP) in Crafting Narratives:

Natural language processing (NLP) stands as the bridge between the raw data and the art of storytelling. In this section, we unravel the magic of NLP algorithms, which empower machines to comprehend, interpret, and generate human-like language. NLP breathes life into the data, allowing for a seamless interaction between consumers and brands.

We explore how NLP analyzes text, understands sentiment, and identifies contextual cues within consumer communications. From chatbots engaging in conversational storytelling to sentiment analysis shaping the emotional tone of narratives, the role of NLP in crafting personalized stories is a testament to the fusion of technology and human expression.

Benefits of AI-Powered Storytelling

1. Efficiency and Scalability:

The marriage of AI and storytelling begets unparalleled efficiency and scalability. Algorithms tirelessly sift through vast datasets, identifying patterns and preferences at a speed beyond human capability. This section outlines how AI streamlines the content creation process, allowing for the rapid generation of personalized narratives tailored to each individual.

As we explore case studies of brands leveraging AI for efficiency, we witness the transformation of storytelling from a time-intensive process to a dynamic and scalable endeavor. The efficiency gained through AI algorithms empowers marketers to engage with a global audience without compromising the depth of personalization.

2. Enhanced Emotional Resonance:

At the heart of AI-powered storytelling lies the capacity to understand and evoke emotions. This section delves into how algorithms analyze emotional cues, enabling the creation of narratives that resonate on a deeply emotional level. From identifying sentiment in customer feedback to adapting storytelling based on emotional triggers, AI amplifies the emotional resonance of brand stories.

Real-world examples demonstrate how AI algorithms decipher the emotional nuances of consumer interactions, contributing to narratives that not only capture attention but also forge lasting emotional connections. The synergy between technology and emotion becomes the secret ingredient for stories that transcend the digital divide.

3. Improved Customer Engagement and Loyalty:

The transformative power of AI extends beyond efficiency and emotional resonance to redefine customer engagement and loyalty. This section explores how personalized storytelling, driven by AI algorithms, becomes a catalyst for sustained customer relationships. By tailoring content to individual preferences, brands cultivate a sense of connection and understanding.

Case studies showcase how AI contributes to personalized customer journeys, resulting in heightened engagement and increased brand loyalty. From adaptive content recommendations to anticipatory storytelling, the narrative unfolds with examples of how AI transforms sporadic transactions into ongoing, meaningful relationships.

The realm of AI algorithms, we uncover how these technologies decipher the intricacies of consumer behavior, learning from past interactions to predict future preferences

In the ever-evolving realm of AI algorithms, we embark on a journey to unravel the intricate dance between technology and the nuances of consumer behavior. These algorithms, fueled by the power of machine learning and deep learning, possess the remarkable ability to decipher the complexities of individual preferences, learning from past interactions to anticipate and shape future consumer choices.

Understanding Consumer Behavior through AI Algorithms

1. Machine Learning Unveiled:

At the core of AI algorithms lies the transformative force of machine learning. This section provides an insightful exploration into how these algorithms ingest and analyze vast amounts of consumer data. By discerning patterns, correlations, and outliers, machine learning algorithms become adept at understanding the intricacies of consumer behavior.

The narrative unfolds with a deep dive into supervised and unsupervised learning, showcasing how algorithms are trained to recognize the subtle cues that reveal preferences. Through real-world examples, we witness how machine learning algorithms become the digital architects, constructing a personalized understanding of each individual's journey.

2. Deep Learning's In-Depth Understanding:

As we delve further, the narrative ascends to the realm of deep learning sophisticated subset of machine learning. Deep learning algorithms, modeled after the human brain's neural networks, enable a more profound understanding of intricate relationships within consumer data.

This section explores how deep learning excels in recognizing complex patterns and nonlinear dependencies. The narrative is illuminated by examples where deep learning algorithms unveil hidden insights from diverse datasets, providing marketers with a holistic understanding of consumer preferences that extends beyond the surface.

Learning from the Past to Predict the Future:

1. Predictive Analytics:

The story unfolds as we transition from understanding to prediction. AI algorithms, having learned the patterns inherent in historical consumer interactions, turn into predictive engines. This section delves into the mechanics of predictive analytics, where algorithms leverage past behaviors to forecast future preferences.

Through predictive modeling, marketers gain the ability to anticipate what a consumer might desire, guiding the creation of personalized narratives that align with evolving tastes. Real-world applications highlight how businesses harness the foresight provided by these algorithms to stay one step ahead in the ever-changing landscape of consumer preferences.

2. Dynamic Adaptation:

The journey through AI algorithms culminates in the concept of dynamic adaptation. These algorithms, continuously learning and evolving, ensure that narratives remain relevant and resonate with consumers over time. By incorporating feedback loops and real-time data analysis,

AI-driven storytelling adapts to shifts in preferences and emerging trends.

Case studies illustrate the agility of AI algorithms in adjusting storytelling strategies based on evolving consumer behaviors. The narrative concludes by showcasing how this dynamic adaptation is a cornerstone of the symbiotic relationship between brands and consumers, fostering an ongoing dialogue shaped by personalized, anticipatory storytelling.

In the intricate tapestry of AI algorithms, the fusion of machine learning, deep learning, and predictive analytics unveils a landscape where technology not only deciphers but also anticipates the intricacies of consumer behavior. As we journey through this realm, we witness the transformation of data into insights, and insights into stories that resonate deeply with the individual, creating a future where personalized narratives become an intuitive and integral part of the consumer experience.

How NLP analyzes text, understands sentiment, and identifies contextual cues within consumer communications

In the realm of AI-powered personalized storytelling, Natural Language Processing (NLP) stands as a transformative force, empowering machines to not only comprehend but also interpret and generate human-like language. In this chapter, we unravel the magic of NLP algorithms, focusing on how they analyze text, understand sentiment, and identify contextual cues within consumer communications.

Analyzing Text with NLP

1. Tokenization and Parsing:

NLP algorithms begin by breaking down text into smaller units known as tokens. This process, called tokenization, enables the algorithm to understand the structure and syntax of the language. Parsing follows, where the relationships between

44

words are analyzed, forming the foundation for comprehension.

2. Part-of-Speech Tagging:

Understanding the role each word plays in a sentence is crucial. NLP employs part-of-speech tagging to identify whether a word is a noun, verb, adjective, etc. This analysis aids in deciphering the grammatical structure and meaning of the text.

3. Named Entity Recognition (NER):

To add another layer of comprehension, NLP identifies and classifies entities within the text such as names, locations, organizations, and dates. NER enhances the algorithm's ability to grasp the context and significance of specific elements within the communication.

Understanding Sentiment with NLP

1. Sentiment Analysis (Opinion Mining):

Sentiment analysis, a vital component of NLP, focuses on gauging the emotional tone expressed in the text. Through machine learning algorithms, NLP assesses whether the sentiment is positive, negative, or neutral. This analysis is particularly powerful for understanding consumer opinions and attitudes.

2. Emotion Detection:

Moving beyond basic sentiment, advanced NLP algorithms delve into emotion detection. By recognizing emotional cues within the text, these algorithms can discern nuanced feelings, such as joy, anger, sadness, or surprise. This capability adds a layer of depth to understanding the emotional context of consumer communications.

Identifying Contextual Cues within Consumer Communications

1. Contextual Embedding's:

NLP algorithms leverage contextual embedding to understand the meaning of words in relation to their surrounding context. This allows the algorithm to capture the subtle nuances and variations in language, contributing to a more accurate interpretation of consumer communications.

2. Reference Resolution:

Resolving references is essential for understanding who or what pronouns refer to within a text. NLP algorithms employ reference resolution to connect pronouns to their intended entities, ensuring a coherent understanding of the narrative.

3. Contextual Sentiment Analysis:

Contextual sentiment analysis goes beyond basic sentiment analysis by considering the broader context in which the text is situated. NLP algorithms examine the overall narrative, ensuring that sentiments expressed in different parts of the text are interpreted in light of the broader story.

47

Real-World Applications and Case Studies

Customer Feedback Analysis:

Illustrative examples demonstrate how NLP is applied to analyze customer feedback, extracting valuable insights regarding product satisfaction, pain points, and areas of improvement.

Social Media Listening:

Case studies showcase how NLP is employed in social media listening, enabling brands to understand public sentiment, identify trends, and respond to consumer conversations in real time.

Chatbot Interactions:

Examining how NLP powers chatbots, creating conversational interfaces that understand and respond to user queries in natural language.

Ethical Considerations and Challenges

Bias Detection:

NLP algorithms must address and mitigate biases present in the data to ensure fair and unbiased analysis.

Privacy Concerns:

The responsible use of NLP in handling sensitive consumer communications and respecting privacy considerations.

Continual Improvement

The need for ongoing refinement and improvement of NLP algorithms to keep pace with evolving language patterns and cultural shifts.

As we navigate the capabilities of NLP in analyzing text, understanding sentiment, and identifying contextual cues within consumer communications, we witness the transformative impact of these algorithms on the personalization and emotional resonance of AI-powered storytelling. The

synergy between technology and language becomes a gateway to crafting narratives that not only understand but also authentically connect with the diverse voices of consumers.

How AI streamlines the content creation process, allowing for the rapid generation of personalized narratives tailored to each individual

CHAPTER 3

STREAMLINING CONTENT CREATION WITH AI IN PERSONALIZED STORYTELLING

In this chapter, we delve into the transformative role of artificial intelligence (AI) in streamlining the content creation process, ushering in an era where personalized narratives are rapidly generated to cater to the unique preferences and behaviors of each individual.

Data-Driven Insights

1. Understanding Individual Preferences:

AI algorithms analyze vast datasets to decipher individual preferences based on past interactions and behaviors.

Data-driven insights serve as the foundation for crafting narratives that resonate with each individual on a personal level.

2. Segmentation and Personalization:

AI enables the segmentation of audiences into distinct groups based on their preferences and characteristics.

Personalized narratives are tailored to specific segments, ensuring relevance and engagement.

Efficient Content Generation

1. Automated Copywriting:

AI-driven tools, equipped with natural language processing capabilities, automate the generation of creative and compelling copy.

Marketers leverage automated copywriting to efficiently create personalized messages for various segments.

2. Dynamic Content Templates:

AI allows for the creation of dynamic content templates that can be customized on the fly.

Templates adapt to individual preferences, ensuring that each narrative is uniquely tailored.

Adaptive Storytelling

1. Real-Time Personalization:

AI algorithms operate in real-time, adapting narratives based on immediate user interactions.

Adaptive storytelling ensures that the content remains relevant and resonant as consumer preferences evolve.

2. Contextual Relevance:

AI considers contextual cues, such as current user behavior or external factors, to dynamically adjust storytelling.

Narratives seamlessly integrate into the context of each consumer's journey, enhancing overall relevance.

Multichannel Consistency

1. Unified Brand Story:

AI ensures consistency in storytelling across various channels and platforms.

A unified brand story is maintained, providing a coherent experience for consumers across diverse touchpoints.

2. Optimized Delivery Timing:

AI algorithms analyze consumer behavior to determine optimal times for content delivery.

Personalized narratives are delivered when individuals are most receptive, enhancing engagement.

Creative Assistance

1. Content Ideation and Creation:

AI-powered tools assist marketers in ideating and creating content by analyzing trending topics and consumer preferences.

54

Creativity is augmented, and content creation becomes a collaborative effort between humans and AI.

2. Visual and Multimedia Enhancement:

AI enhances visual and multimedia elements within narratives, ensuring a captivating and personalized user experience.

The fusion of AI-driven visuals with personalized narratives elevates the emotional impact of storytelling.

Performance Optimization

1. Data-Driven Iterations:

AI continually analyzes performance metrics and user feedback to iterate and optimize content.

Marketers leverage data insights to refine and enhance narratives for ongoing effectiveness.

2. A/B Testing Automation:

A/B testing is automated through AI algorithms, allowing for rapid experimentation with different narrative elements.

Iterative testing ensures continuous improvement in the effectiveness of personalized storytelling.

Ethical Considerations

1. Transparency and Consent:

Ensuring transparency in AI-driven content creation processes and obtaining user consent for personalized experiences.

Ethical considerations guide the responsible use of AI to enhance user trust.

2. Mitigating Algorithmic Bias:

Implementing measures to detect and mitigate biases in AI algorithms to ensure fair and unbiased content generation.

Ongoing monitoring and adjustments contribute to ethical and inclusive storytelling practices.

As we navigate the landscape of AI-driven content creation, the efficiencies gained in the process allow for the rapid generation of personalized narratives tailored to each individual. The marriage of data-driven insights, automation, and adaptive storytelling ushers in an era where brands can authentically connect with their audience on a personal level, fostering deeper engagement and loyalty.

CHAPTER 4

ANALYZING EMOTIONAL CUES FOR DEEP EMOTIONAL RESONANCE IN PERSONALIZED STORYTELLING

In this chapter, we explore how algorithms harness the power of emotional analysis to create narratives that resonate on a profoundly emotional level. Understanding emotional cues is a critical aspect of AI-powered personalized storytelling, allowing for the crafting of narratives that connect with individuals on a deeply emotional and personal level.

Emotion Recognition Technologies

1. Facial Expression Analysis:

Algorithms utilize facial recognition technology to analyze expressions and identify emotional cues.

By detecting micro-expressions, the system gauges emotional responses in real-time, providing valuable insights into the user's emotional state.

2. Voice and Tone Analysis:

Speech analysis algorithms assess nuances in tone, pitch, and pacing to identify emotional undertones.

Understanding the emotional nuances in voice contributes to the creation of narratives that align with the user's current emotional state.

3. Textual Sentiment Analysis:

Natural Language Processing (NLP) algorithms analyze text for sentiment, identifying emotional cues expressed in written communication.

Sentiment analysis tools categorize language as positive, negative, or neutral, providing a basis for emotional understanding.

Mapping Emotional Responses

1. Emotional Mapping of Interactions:

Algorithms map emotional responses to specific content and interactions.

Through machine learning, the system learns which elements evoke positive or negative emotions, refining its emotional intelligence over time.

2. Contextual Emotional Analysis:

Algorithms consider the contextual relevance of emotional cues within the user's journey.

Understanding the broader context allows for the creation of emotionally resonant narratives that align with the user's experiences and expectations.

Dynamic Content Adaptation

1. Real-Time Adjustments Based on Emotional State:

AI algorithms dynamically adapt content based on the user's current emotional state.

Real-time adjustments ensure that the narrative evolves to maintain emotional resonance throughout the user's journey.

2. Emotion-Triggered Personalization:

Emotional cues serve as triggers for personalized content recommendations.

The system anticipates the user's emotional needs and tailors narratives that address and complement their emotional state.

Creating Emotionally Resonant Narratives

1. Emotionally Intelligent Story Structures:

Algorithms contribute to the design of emotionally intelligent story structures.

Recognizing emotional highs and lows, the system crafts narratives with pacing and content that align with the desired emotional impact.

2. Personalized Emotional Appeals:

Emotional analysis informs the creation of personalized emotional appeals.

By understanding individual preferences in emotional content, the system tailors narratives that align with the user's unique emotional triggers.

Case Studies and Real-World Examples

1. Entertainment Industry:

Explore how streaming platforms leverage emotional analysis to recommend movies or shows based on the viewer's emotional preferences.

Case studies highlight the impact of emotionally resonant content recommendations on user satisfaction and engagement.

2. E-Commerce and Marketing:

Examine how e-commerce platforms use emotional analysis to personalize product recommendations and marketing messages.

Real-world examples showcase the effectiveness of emotionally tailored narratives in driving consumer engagement and conversions.

User Feedback and Iterative Refinement

1. Collecting Emotional Feedback:

Implement strategies for collecting user feedback on emotional responses to content.

Surveys, sentiment analysis, and user interviews contribute to a continuous feedback loop.

2. Iterative Refinement of Emotional Algorithms:

Based on user feedback, continuously refine emotional analysis algorithms.

The iterative process ensures that the system adapts to evolving user preferences and cultural shifts in emotional expression.

Ethical Considerations:

1. Respecting User Privacy:

Address privacy concerns related to emotional data analysis.

Implement transparent policies and obtain user consent for the ethical use of emotional analysis in personalized storytelling.

2. Avoiding Emotional Manipulation:

Establish guidelines to prevent the unethical manipulation of emotions through storytelling.

Striking a balance between emotional resonance and ethical practices ensures a positive user experience.

As we navigate the terrain of emotional analysis in AI-powered personalized storytelling, the fusion of technology and emotional intelligence emerges as a potent force. By understanding and responding to emotional cues, algorithms contribute to the creation of narratives that go beyond information delivery, fostering authentic connections that resonate on a deeply emotional and personal level.

CHAPTER 5

PERSONALIZED STORYTELLING AS A CATALYST FOR SUSTAINED CUSTOMER RELATIONSHIPS

In this chapter, we delve into the transformative role of personalized storytelling, driven by AI algorithms, as a dynamic catalyst for fostering and nurturing sustained customer relationships. The fusion of technology and narrative artistry becomes a powerful force that goes beyond transactional interactions, creating a meaningful and enduring connection between brands and their audience.

Understanding the Foundations

1. Individualized Connection:

Personalized storytelling establishes an individualized connection with each customer.

AI algorithms analyze data to tailor narratives, reflecting the unique preferences, behaviors, and experiences of individuals.

2. Emotional Resonance:

Emotional intelligence embedded in AI algorithms ensures narratives resonate on a deep emotional level.

The emotional resonance becomes a cornerstone for building lasting connections with customers.

Journey Mapping and Continuity

1. Mapping the Customer Journey:

AI-powered personalized storytelling follows customers throughout their journey.

By mapping touchpoints, the narrative adapts to each stage, providing a seamless and continuous brand experience.

2. Consistency across Channels:

Personalized narratives maintain consistency across various channels and platforms.

Customers encounter a unified brand story, reinforcing the brand's identity and message.

Anticipatory Engagement:

1. Predictive Analytics in Action:

AI algorithms use predictive analytics to anticipate customer preferences.

Personalized storytelling becomes anticipatory, offering content and recommendations aligned with future needs and desires.

2. Proactive Storytelling:

Anticipatory engagement enables proactive storytelling.

Brands can initiate narratives that address potential concerns, introduce new products, or celebrate milestones, fostering a proactive relationship with customers.

Adaptive Personalization

1. Real-Time Adaptation:

AI-driven narratives adapt in real-time based on customer interactions.

This adaptive personalization ensures that the storytelling remains relevant and engaging as customer preferences evolve.

2. Feedback Loop Integration:

Customer feedback serves as input for continuous improvement.

The feedback loop is integrated into AI algorithms, refining future personalized narratives and enhancing customer satisfaction.

Enhanced Customer Loyalty

1. Building Trust through Consistency:

Consistent and personalized storytelling builds trust over time.

Trust becomes a foundation for customer loyalty, as individuals feel understood and valued by the brand.

2. Tailored Loyalty Programs:

AI algorithms inform the design of personalized loyalty programs.

Loyalty initiatives are tailored to individual preferences, ensuring rewards align with the unique needs and desires of each customer.

Case Studies and Success Stories

1. E-Commerce Success:

Explore how e-commerce platforms leverage AI-driven personalized storytelling to enhance customer engagement.

Case studies demonstrate the positive impact on customer retention and repeat business.

2. Brand Advocacy through Personalization:

Examine examples of brands that have transformed customers into advocates through personalized storytelling.

The journey from customer satisfaction to brand advocacy showcases the power of personalized narratives in building strong customer relationships.

Long-Term Value Creation

1. Lifetime Value Maximization:

Personalized storytelling contributes to maximizing customer lifetime value.

By adapting to changing preferences and evolving with customers, brands foster a relationship that spans beyond individual transactions.

2. Brand Ambassadorship:

Sustained customer relationships evolve into brand ambassadorship.

Loyal customers who feel emotionally connected become advocates, actively promoting the brand within their networks.

Ethical Considerations

1. Privacy Protection

Emphasize the importance of respecting customer privacy in personalized storytelling.

Clear communication and transparent practices build trust and enhance the ethical standing of the brand.

2. Balancing Personalization and Intrusiveness:

Address the delicate balance between personalization and avoiding intrusiveness.

Ethical guidelines ensure that the personalized storytelling experience enhances customer relationships without crossing privacy boundaries.

As we navigate the realm of personalized storytelling fueled by AI algorithms, the narrative emerges as more than a marketing tool it becomes a catalyst for building sustained and meaningful relationships with customers. Through emotional resonance, anticipatory engagement, and adaptive personalization, brands create an immersive and enduring experience that goes beyond the transactional, nurturing loyalty and advocacy over the long term.

CHAPTER 6

DEVELOPING AI ALGORITHMS FOR PERSONALIZED STORYTELLING

In this chapter, we delve into the intricacies of developing AI algorithms for personalized storytelling. The foundation of crafting emotionally resonant brand stories rests on a data-driven approach and a thoughtful design that understands and incorporates emotional triggers responsibly.

Data-Driven Approach

1. Utilizing Consumer Data for Algorithm Development:

a. Data Collection Strategies: - Explore diverse sources of consumer data, including online behavior, purchase history, social interactions, and demographic information. - Develop a comprehensive data collection strategy that ensures the

74

richness and relevance of the dataset for algorithm training.

b. Advanced Analytics: - Employ advanced analytics techniques, including machine learning and data mining, to extract meaningful patterns and insights. - Implement algorithms that can process and analyze large datasets efficiently, uncovering nuanced consumer preferences and behaviors.

c. Behavior Prediction: - Leverage historical consumer data to predict future behaviors. - Develop algorithms that can anticipate individual preferences, allowing for the proactive tailoring of brand stories based on predicted needs.

2. Ensuring Ethical and Responsible Use of Data:

a. Privacy by Design: - Embed privacy considerations into the algorithm development process from the outset. - Implement privacy-preserving techniques, such as data anonymization and secure data storage, to safeguard consumer information.

b. Transparency and Consent: - Establish transparent communication with consumers regarding data usage. - Prioritize obtaining explicit consent for personalized storytelling, ensuring customers are aware of how their data is being utilized.

c. Algorithmic Bias Mitigation: - Implement measures to detect and mitigate biases in the data that could lead to unfair or discriminatory outcomes. - Regularly audit algorithms to ensure fairness, transparency, and inclusivity in personalized storytelling.

Designing Emotionally Resonant Narratives

1. Understanding Emotional Triggers:

a. Psychological Insights: - Collaborate with psychologists and emotion experts to understand the psychological nuances of emotional triggers. - Utilize this insight to identify emotions that resonate most strongly with the target audience.

b. Data-Driven Emotional Analysis: - Incorporate emotional analysis algorithms to identify and understand emotional cues in consumer interactions. - Analyze how consumers respond emotionally to different storytelling elements and identify patterns that inform future narrative design.

c. Cultural Sensitivity: - Consider cultural nuances when identifying emotional triggers, ensuring narratives are culturally sensitive and resonate authentically with diverse audiences. - Adapt emotional triggers based on cultural preferences and differences.

2. Incorporating Storytelling Elements for Maximum Impact:

a. Personalization through Narratives: - Develop algorithms that enable dynamic personalization within narratives, tailoring content based on individual preferences. - Utilize consumer data to create personalized story arcs that align with individual journeys.

b. Visual and Multimedia Enhancement: - Integrate AI-driven visual elements that enhance emotional impact, such as emotionally expressive visuals or interactive multimedia. - Utilize algorithms to analyze the effectiveness of different visual elements in eliciting emotional responses.

c. Dynamic Story Structures: - Implement algorithms that adapt story structures in real-time based on user engagement and emotional responses. - Explore nonlinear storytelling approaches that dynamically evolve to maintain engagement and emotional resonance.

Case Studies and Real-World Examples

a. Successful Implementations: - Explore case studies of brands that have effectively developed AI algorithms for personalized storytelling. - Highlight the positive impact on consumer engagement, brand loyalty, and overall marketing effectiveness.

b. Challenges and Learning Experiences: - Discuss challenges faced by brands in the development and implementation of AI algorithms for personalized storytelling. - Share insights and lessons learned from real-world experiences, emphasizing the importance of adaptability and continual refinement.

Ethical Considerations

a. Empowering Users: - Implement user controls that allow individuals to customize the level of personalization they are comfortable with. - Educate users about the value exchange in personalized storytelling and how their data contributes to a more tailored and relevant experience.

b. Guardrails for Algorithmic Decisions: - Establish ethical guidelines that define the limits of algorithmic decision-making in storytelling. - Ensure algorithms prioritize user well-being and avoid manipulative practices.

c. Continuous Ethical Review: - Integrate continuous ethical reviews into the algorithm development process. - Periodically reassess algorithms to align with evolving ethical standards and address emerging concerns.

In conclusion, developing AI algorithms for personalized storytelling requires a holistic approach that embraces a data-driven foundation, an understanding of emotional triggers, and a commitment to ethical and responsible use. By leveraging consumer data ethically and designing narratives that resonate emotionally, brands can create compelling, tailored stories that foster deep connections and sustained relationships with their audience.

CHAPTER 7

CASE STUDIES

In this chapter, we delve into real-world case studies to examine successful implementations of AI-powered personalized storytelling. Through the experiences of notable brands, we explore lessons learned, best practices, and the transformative impact of leveraging AI algorithms to craft emotionally resonant brand stories based on individual consumer preferences and behavior.

Successful Implementations of AI-Powered Personalized Storytelling

1. Netflix: Tailoring Content for Individual Tastes:

a. Personalized Recommendations: - Netflix employs advanced AI algorithms to analyze viewing history, preferences, and user behavior. - The platform provides

81

personalized content recommendations, tailoring the user experience to individual tastes.

b. Dynamic Story Thumbnails: AI-driven dynamic story thumbnails adapt based on user engagement and preferences. - By analyzing which visuals resonate most effectively, Netflix optimizes the presentation of content to capture viewer attention.

c. User Engagement Impact: Explore the impact of personalized storytelling on user engagement and retention. - Lessons learned from Netflix's approach to continuously refining algorithms for improved content personalization.

2. Spotify: Crafting Personalized Soundtracks:

a. AI-Powered Playlist Recommendations: - Spotify leverages AI to curate personalized playlists based on user listening history and preferences. - Discover how algorithms dynamically adjust playlists in real-time to align with changing musical tastes.

B. Podcast Recommendations: - AI algorithms extend to recommending podcasts tailored to individual interests and behaviors. - Spotify's case study highlights the nuances of personalizing narratives within audio content.

c. User Satisfaction and Retention: - Examine the impact of personalized storytelling on user satisfaction and long-term platform loyalty. - Insights into how Spotify uses algorithmic personalization to maintain a competitive edge in the music streaming industry.

Lessons Learned and Best Practices

1. Iterative Algorithm Refinement:

a. Continuous Learning: - Both Netflix and Spotify showcase the importance of continuous learning through iterative algorithm refinement. - Explore how regular adjustments based on user feedback and evolving preferences contribute to enhanced personalization.

b. Agile Development Approaches: - Agile development methodologies are essential for adapting algorithms swiftly to changing consumer behaviors. - Best practices emphasize the agility required to stay ahead in the dynamic landscape of personalized storytelling.

2. Balancing Personalization and Privacy:

a. User Empowerment: - Netflix and Spotify prioritize user empowerment, allowing individuals to control the extent of personalization. - Lessons learned from implementing features that give users the ability to influence their own storytelling experience.

b. Transparent Communication: - Transparent communication about data usage and personalization strategies fosters trust. - Examine how brands navigate the delicate balance between personalization and user privacy while maintaining transparency.

3. Dynamic Adaptation to Cultural Shifts:

a. Cultural Sensitivity: - Cultural nuances significantly impact the success of personalized storytelling. - Learn from case studies about how brands incorporate dynamic adaptations to align with evolving cultural shifts, ensuring narratives remain relevant.

b. Global Success Stories: - Netflix and Spotify's global success stories highlight the effectiveness of tailoring narratives to diverse audiences. - Best practices for navigating cultural diversity and ensuring resonant storytelling across different regions.

4. User-Generated Content Integration:

a. Interactive Storytelling: - Both platforms explore interactive storytelling features that allow users to influence the narrative. - Best practices for integrating user-generated content and fostering a sense of co-creation in personalized storytelling.

b. Community Building: - Spotify and Netflix leverage user interactions to build communities around shared interests. - Explore how community-building aspects contribute to the success of personalized storytelling platforms.

Implications for Future Personalized Storytelling

1. Emerging Trends and Technologies:

a. AI Advancements: - Discuss emerging trends in AI that are poised to further enhance personalized storytelling. - Explore the potential impact of advancements in machine learning, natural language processing, and emotional intelligence.

b. Immersive Technologies: - Consider the integration of immersive technologies, such as virtual reality (VR) and augmented reality (AR), in personalized storytelling. - Lessons learned from early adopters and the potential for creating immersive, personalized brand experiences.

2. Ethical Considerations and Responsible AI:

a. User Privacy and Data Security: - Ongoing commitment to user privacy and data security is crucial for the sustained success of personalized storytelling platforms. - Best practices for addressing ethical considerations and maintaining responsible AI practices.

b. Guardrails for Algorithmic Decisions: - As AI algorithms play a central role, establishing clear guardrails for algorithmic decisions becomes paramount. - Lessons learned from navigating ethical considerations in algorithmic storytelling.

Closing Thoughts

1. The Transformative Power of Personalized Storytelling:

a. Brand-Consumer Relationships: - Reflect on how personalized storytelling, driven by AI algorithms, transforms brand-consumer relationships. - The profound impact on customer loyalty, brand advocacy, and the future of marketing.

2. Continual Evolution and Innovation:

a. The Journey Ahead: Conclude with a look toward the future of personalized storytelling. Emphasize the need for continual evolution, innovation, and a commitment to creating narratives that authentically connect with individuals.

CHAPTER 8

CHALLENGES AND ETHICAL CONSIDERATIONS

In this chapter, we confront the challenges and ethical considerations associated with AI-powered personalized storytelling. As brands strive to create emotionally resonant narratives based on individual consumer preferences and behaviors, it becomes imperative to address privacy concerns, maintain transparency, and strike a balance between personalization and diversity and inclusion.

Privacy Concerns

1. Safeguarding Consumer Information:

a. Data Encryption and Security Measures: Explore advanced data encryption techniques to safeguard consumer information from unauthorized access. -

Implement robust security measures to ensure the integrity and confidentiality of personal data.

b. Secure Data Storage Practices: - Discuss best practices for secure data storage, minimizing the risk of data breaches or leaks. - Emphasize the importance of regularly updating security protocols to stay ahead of evolving cyber threats.

2. Transparency in Data Usage:

a. Consumer Education: - Implement clear and comprehensive communication strategies to educate consumers on how their data is used. - Emphasize the importance of obtaining informed consent and providing consumers with the ability to control their data preferences.

b. Data Usage Policies: - Establish transparent data usage policies that outline the purposes and scope of data collection. - Case studies highlighting successful communication strategies that build trust and confidence in consumers regarding data usage.

c. Opt-In Mechanisms: - Advocate for opt-in mechanisms that empower users to actively participate in personalized storytelling. - Examine how brands can leverage opt-in features to enhance transparency and build a foundation of trust.

Balancing Personalization with Diversity and Inclusion

1. Avoiding Algorithmic Bias:

a. Algorithmic Audits and Bias Detection: - Propose the implementation of regular algorithmic audits to detect and rectify biases in AI algorithms. - Explore the use of specialized tools and techniques designed to identify and mitigate bias in personalized storytelling algorithms.

b. Diverse Training Data: - Emphasize the importance of using diverse training data that accurately represents the full spectrum of consumer demographics. - Discuss strategies for curating datasets that account for cultural, ethnic, and socio-economic diversity.

c. Explainable AI: - Introduce the concept of explainable AI, enabling users and developers to understand the decision-making processes of algorithms. - Evaluate the role of explain ability in building trust and mitigating concerns related to biased outcomes.

2. Ensuring Representation in Personalized Stories:

a. Cultural Competence in Storytelling: - Highlight the significance of cultural competence in crafting personalized stories that resonate with diverse audiences. - Showcase examples of brands that have successfully embraced cultural inclusivity in their narratives.

b. User-Generated Content and Co-Creation: Encourage user-generated content and co-creation strategies to ensure diverse perspectives are incorporated into personalized stories. - Examine case studies illustrating the positive impact of collaborative storytelling approaches.

c. Accessibility Considerations: - Address accessibility concerns to ensure that personalized stories are inclusive and accessible to individuals with diverse needs. - Discuss how brands can incorporate accessibility features to enhance the inclusivity of their storytelling platforms.

Implications for Ethical Personalized Storytelling

1. Ethical Decision-Making Frameworks:

a. **Establishing Ethical Guidelines:** - Advocate for the development and implementation of ethical decision-making frameworks within AI algorithms. - Explore how brands can establish guidelines that prioritize user well-being, fairness, and transparency.

2. User Empowerment and Control:

a. **Empowering Users:** - Discuss the role of user empowerment in ethical personalized storytelling. - Examine features that allow users to control the level of personalization they experience, fostering a sense of agency.

b. Feedback Mechanisms: - Implementing feedback mechanisms that enable users to provide insights into the impact and appropriateness of personalized stories. - Explore how user feedback contributes to iterative improvements and ethical refinements.

The Road Ahead

1. Continual Monitoring and Adaptation:

a. Ongoing Ethical Reviews: - Propose the incorporation of continual ethical reviews into the development and deployment of personalized storytelling algorithms. - Discuss the importance of staying vigilant and adaptive to emerging ethical considerations.

2. Collaboration and Industry Standards:

a. Cross-Industry Collaboration: - Advocate for collaboration between industries to establish ethical standards and best practices for personalized storytelling. - Explore the potential for industry-wide

94

initiatives that prioritize ethical considerations in AI-driven narratives.

3. Public Discourse and Awareness:

a. Educating the Public: - Highlight the role of public discourse and awareness in shaping ethical standards. - Discuss strategies for engaging with the public, addressing concerns, and fostering a collective understanding of responsible AI practices.

4. Incorporating Ethical Considerations into Design:

a. Ethical Design Thinking: - Integrate ethical considerations into the design thinking process for personalized storytelling platforms. - Examine how ethical design thinking ensures that values of inclusivity, fairness, and user empowerment are embedded in the core of algorithmic development.

Closing Thoughts

1. Ethical Foundations of AI-Powered Personalized Storytelling:

a. The Moral Imperative: - Conclude with the assertion that ethical considerations are not just a legal requirement but a moral imperative in the realm of AI-powered personalized storytelling. - Emphasize the transformative potential of ethical practices in fostering trust, building lasting relationships, and creating narratives that resonate responsibly with diverse audiences.

CHAPTER 9

FUTURE TRENDS IN AI-POWERED PERSONALIZED STORYTELLING

In this chapter, we explore the exciting frontier of AI-powered personalized storytelling, considering the advances in AI technology and the evolving landscape of consumer expectations. As brands embark on a journey to craft emotionally resonant narratives based on individual preferences, understanding and anticipating these future trends become crucial for staying at the forefront of storytelling innovation.

Advances in AI Technology

1. Predictive Algorithms:

a. Anticipating User Needs: - Delve into the realm of predictive algorithms that go beyond understanding current preferences to anticipate future needs. - Explore how algorithms can leverage historical data to predict evolving consumer behaviors, enabling proactive and personalized storytelling.

b. Dynamic Content Prediction: - Discuss the evolution of algorithms in predicting the type of content that will resonate with individual users at specific points in their journey. - Explore case studies illustrating the impact of dynamic content prediction on user engagement and satisfaction.

2. Integration with Emerging Technologies (e.g., Augmented Reality):

a. Augmented Reality (AR) and Immersive Experiences: - Examine the integration of AI-powered personalized storytelling with emerging technologies like augmented reality. - Discuss how AR enhances the immersive nature of personalized narratives, offering users a more interactive and visually compelling experience.

B. Cross-Platform Integration: - Explore how personalized storytelling can

98

seamlessly transition across various platforms, integrating AR experiences into both online and offline brand interactions. - Consider the potential of AR to revolutionize the way brands tell stories and connect with consumers in real-world environments.

c. Virtual Reality (VR) and Storytelling Immersion: - Discuss the potential of virtual reality in creating highly immersive and emotionally resonant personalized narratives. - Explore how AI algorithms can adapt storytelling elements to suit the unique characteristics of VR environments, providing users with unparalleled experiences.

Evolving Consumer Expectations

1. Shifting Preferences and Demands:

a. Real-Time Adaptability: - Examine the need for real-time adaptability in personalized storytelling to keep pace with rapidly changing consumer preferences. - Discuss how AI algorithms can dynamically adjust narratives based on real-time data, ensuring continuous relevance.

b. Hyper-Personalization: - Explore the concept of hyper-personalization, where narratives are tailored to an unprecedented level of granularity. - Discuss the challenges and opportunities associated with delivering personalized stories that cater to the minutiae of individual preferences.

2. Staying Ahead of the Curve in Storytelling Innovation:

a. Agile Storytelling Frameworks: - Propose the adoption of agile storytelling frameworks that allow brands to quickly iterate and experiment with narrative approaches. - Highlight case studies of brands that have successfully implemented agile methodologies to stay ahead in the rapidly evolving landscape.

b. Innovative Interactive Elements: - Discuss the incorporation of innovative interactive elements within personalized narratives to enhance engagement. - Explore how gamification, interactive decision points, and participatory storytelling contribute to a more immersive user experience.

c. **User-Generated and Co-Created Narratives:** - Emphasize the trend towards user-generated and co-created narratives, where consumers actively participate in the storytelling process. - Showcase examples of brands that have successfully embraced co-creation, fostering a sense of community and shared storytelling.

Implications for Brands and Marketers

1. Adapting Organizational Structures:

a. **Agile Marketing Teams:** - Discuss the need for agile marketing teams capable of quickly responding to emerging trends in personalized storytelling. - Explore how organizational structures can be adapted to facilitate innovation and collaboration in storytelling practices.

2. Investing in AI Talent and Expertise:

a. AI-Driven Marketing Roles: - Highlight the emergence of specialized roles within marketing focused on AI-driven storytelling. - Discuss the importance of investing in talent and expertise to effectively leverage AI technologies for personalized narratives.

3. Ethical Considerations in Future Innovations:

a. Anticipating Ethical Challenges: - Acknowledge potential ethical challenges associated with future innovations in AI-powered personalized storytelling. - Discuss proactive measures brands can take to address ethical concerns and maintain user trust.

Collaboration and Industry Trends

1. Cross-Industry Collaboration:

a. Knowledge Sharing: - Advocate for cross-industry collaboration and knowledge sharing to accelerate innovations in personalized storytelling. - Explore how collaboration can lead to the development of industry standards and best practices.

2. The Role of Industry Associations:

a. Guidance and Standards: - Examine the potential role of industry associations in providing guidance and setting standards for AI-powered personalized storytelling. - Discuss the benefits of collective efforts in navigating ethical considerations and technological advancements.

Closing Thoughts

1. The Ever-Evolving Landscape of Personalized Storytelling:

a. Continuous Evolution: - Conclude by emphasizing the dynamic nature of personalized storytelling, driven by advances in AI technology and evolving consumer expectations. - Emphasize the need for brands to maintain a mindset of continuous evolution and adaptation to remain at the forefront of storytelling innovation.

2. The Human Touch in the Age of AI:

a. Balancing Technology and Humanity: - Reflect on the delicate balance between technological innovation and the fundamental human aspects of storytelling. - Emphasize the enduring importance of authenticity, empathy, and emotional connection in crafting narratives that resonate deeply with individuals.

104

CHAPTER 10

IMPLEMENTATION STRATEGIES

In this chapter, we delve into actionable steps for businesses to adopt AI-powered personalized storytelling successfully. From building a skilled AI team to seamlessly integrating these strategies with existing marketing approaches, the implementation process is crucial for harnessing the transformative power of AI in crafting personalized and emotionally resonant brand stories.

Steps for Businesses to Adopt AI-Powered Personalized Storytelling

1. Building a Skilled AI Team:

a. AI Talent Acquisition: - Discuss the importance of recruiting skilled professionals in the fields of artificial intelligence, machine learning, and data science. - Explore strategies for identifying and attracting top talent with expertise in developing and implementing AI algorithms.

b. Cross-Functional Collaboration: - Advocate for cross-functional collaboration between AI experts, marketing professionals, and data analysts. - Highlight the benefits of a diverse team that combines technical expertise with a deep understanding of marketing and consumer behavior.

c. Continuous Training and Development: - Emphasize the need for ongoing training and development programs to keep the AI team abreast of the latest advancements in technology. - Explore avenues for upskilling and reskilling team members to ensure a dynamic and adaptive workforce.

d. Ethical Considerations Training: - Integrate ethical considerations training into the AI team's curriculum. - Discuss the importance of fostering a culture that prioritizes responsible AI practices and ethical storytelling.

2. Integration with Existing Marketing Strategies:

a. Audit of Current Marketing Practices: - Conduct a comprehensive audit of existing marketing strategies to identify areas where AI-powered personalized storytelling can be seamlessly integrated. - Assess the alignment of current practices with the goals of personalization, engagement, and emotional resonance.

b. Data Integration and Management: - Streamline data integration by connecting disparate data sources to create a unified view of consumer preferences and behaviors. - Discuss data management best practices to ensure the quality, security, and accessibility of data for AI algorithms.

c. Pilot Programs and Incremental Implementation: - Propose the implementation of pilot programs to test the effectiveness of AI-powered personalized storytelling on a smaller scale. - Highlight the benefits of incremental implementation, allowing businesses to learn, adapt, and refine strategies before full-scale deployment.

d. Collaboration Across Departments: - Encourage collaboration across various departments, including marketing, IT, and customer support, to ensure a holistic approach to personalized storytelling. - Discuss the role of interdepartmental communication in aligning AI initiatives with overall business objectives.

e. User Feedback Integration: - Emphasize the importance of integrating user feedback into the AI-powered personalized storytelling process. - Explore strategies for collecting and analyzing user feedback to inform iterative improvements and enhance the user experience.

Case Studies and Real-World Examples

a. Successful Adoption Stories: - Explore case studies of businesses that have successfully adopted AI-powered personalized storytelling. - Highlight the challenges faced, lessons learned, and the transformative impact on customer engagement and brand perception.

b. Diverse Industry Applications: - Showcase examples from diverse industries, including e-commerce, entertainment, and healthcare, illustrating the versatility of AI-powered personalized storytelling. - Discuss the unique challenges and opportunities each industry faces in implementation.

Measurement and Analytics

1. Defining Key Performance Indicators (KPIs):

a. Identifying Metrics for Success: - Work with the AI team to define key performance indicators (KPIs) aligned with the goals of personalized storytelling. - Discuss metrics such as user engagement, conversion rates, and customer satisfaction as benchmarks for success.

b. Real-Time Analytics: - Explore the integration of real-time analytics tools to monitor the performance of personalized storytelling campaigns. - Discuss the advantages of real-time insights in adapting strategies on the fly and maximizing impact.

c. Attribution Modeling: - Implement attribution modeling to understand the contribution of personalized storytelling to overall marketing success. - Discuss how businesses can accurately attribute outcomes to personalized narratives in a multichannel marketing environment.

Ethical Considerations and User Trust

1. Transparent Communication:

a. User-Friendly Explanations: - Emphasize the importance of transparent communication with users about the use of AI in crafting personalized stories. - Discuss strategies for providing user-friendly explanations that demystify the technology and build trust.

b. Privacy Protection Measures: - Outline the privacy protection measures implemented to reassure users about the responsible use of their data. - Discuss the role of clear privacy policies and consent mechanisms in maintaining ethical storytelling practices.

c. Feedback Channels for Ethical Concerns: - Establish accessible channels for users to express ethical concerns related to personalized storytelling. - Discuss the benefits of creating an open dialogue with users to address concerns and continuously refine ethical practices.

Scalability and Future-Proofing

1. Scalability Considerations:

a. Infrastructure Readiness: - Assess the scalability of existing infrastructure to accommodate the growth of AI-powered personalized storytelling initiatives. - Explore strategies for ensuring that technical resources can scale with increasing demands.

b. Automated Processes for Efficiency: - Advocate for the automation of processes wherever possible to enhance efficiency and scalability. - Discuss the benefits of automated content generation, data analysis, and user interactions in maintaining scalability.

2. Future-Proofing Strategies:

a. Adapting to Technological Advancements: - Discuss strategies for future-proofing AI-powered personalized storytelling initiatives by staying adaptable to emerging technologies. - Explore the integration of modular and flexible solutions that can evolve with advancements in AI and related fields.

b. Continuous Learning and Innovation: - Highlight the importance of a culture of continuous learning and innovation within the organization. - Discuss how businesses can foster an environment that encourages experimentation, creativity, and staying ahead of industry trends.

Closing Thoughts

1. The Transformative Potential of Implementation:

a. From Vision to Reality: - Conclude by emphasizing that the true transformative potential of AI-powered personalized storytelling is realized through effective implementation. - Encourage businesses to embark on this journey with a strategic, collaborative, and ethical approach to create narratives that resonate deeply with individual consumers.

Dynamic Future Awaits

As we look ahead, a dynamic and transformative future awaits in the realm of AI-powered personalized storytelling. This concluding section explores the exciting possibilities and potential developments that lie on the horizon.

1. Hyper-Personalization Unleashed:

Envision a future where hyper-personalization becomes the norm rather than the exception.

Discuss the potential for AI algorithms to delve even deeper into individual preferences, tailoring narratives to the minutest nuances of a person's tastes, behaviors, and emotions.

2. Immersive Experiences with Extended Reality (XR):

Explore the integration of extended reality (XR) technologies, such as augmented

113

reality (AR) and virtual reality (VR), into personalized storytelling.

Envision immersive experiences where consumers engage with brands in virtual spaces, blurring the lines between the physical and digital worlds.

3. Predictive Narratives with Advanced Algorithms:

Envisage a future where AI algorithms evolve to not only understand current preferences but predict future desires.

Discuss the potential of predictive algorithms to anticipate user needs, delivering personalized narratives that align with consumers' evolving tastes and aspirations.

4. Seamless Cross-Platform Integration:

Explore a landscape where personalized storytelling seamlessly transitions across diverse platforms.

Envision narratives that effortlessly adapt to different channels, including social media, mobile apps, websites, and physical spaces, creating a cohesive brand experience.

5. Conversational Storytelling with AI Chatbots:

Delve into the realm of conversational storytelling facilitated by AI-powered chatbots.

Envision consumers engaging in dynamic conversations with AI interfaces, receiving personalized stories that unfold based on real-time interactions and responses.

6. Interactive and Participatory Narratives:

Envision narratives that transcend traditional storytelling, inviting consumers to actively participate in the co-creation of brand stories.

Explore the potential for interactive elements, gamification, and collaborative storytelling approaches that foster a sense of community and engagement.

7. Ethical AI at the Core:

Highlight the growing importance of ethical AI practices as a cornerstone of personalized storytelling.

Discuss industry-wide commitments to transparency, user empowerment, and responsible data usage, ensuring that ethical considerations remain central to the development and deployment of AI algorithms.

8. Continued Collaboration and Innovation:

Emphasize the need for continued collaboration across industries and a commitment to innovation.

Envision a future where businesses share knowledge, best practices, and collectively drive the evolution of AI-powered personalized storytelling.

9. A Global Tapestry of Inclusive Stories:

Picture a future where personalized storytelling contributes to a rich global tapestry of inclusive narratives.

Advocate for diverse voices, cultures, and perspectives being authentically represented in brand stories, fostering a sense of connection and understanding among a wide range of audiences.

10. Empowered Consumers Shaping Narratives:

Envision a landscape where consumers are not just recipients but active shapers of brand narratives.

Discuss the potential for consumers to have greater control and influence, co-creating stories that resonate with their values, preferences, and aspirations.

In this dynamic future, AI-powered personalized storytelling has the potential to redefine how businesses connect with consumers, fostering deeper relationships and creating memorable experiences. As businesses embrace this transformative journey, the key lies not just in the technological advancements but in the delicate balance between technology and the human touch. The tapestry of stories that unfold will be as diverse as the individuals they engage, weaving a narrative of innovation, inclusivity, and a harmonious blend of artificial intelligence and human emotion. The future is dynamic, and as we embrace the possibilities, the storytelling landscape is poised for an exciting and enriching evolution.

CHAPTER 11

CONCLUSION

In this concluding chapter, we reflect on the key concepts explored in "AI-Powered Personalized Storytelling: Develop AI algorithms that craft personalized and emotionally resonant brand stories based on individual consumer preferences and behavior." We present a compelling call to action for businesses to embrace AI-powered personalized storytelling and envision the future of marketing and brand communication in this transformative landscape.

Recap of Key Concepts:

1. The Power of Personalization:

Recap the significance of personalized storytelling in marketing, emphasizing its ability to create emotionally resonant connections with individual consumers.

Highlight the role of AI in elevating personalization to new heights by

119

leveraging data-driven insights and predictive algorithms.

2. Understanding Consumer Behavior:

Summarize the exploration of consumer preferences, behavioral patterns, and the methodologies employed in data collection and analysis.

Emphasize the importance of unraveling the psychology behind consumer preferences, from socio-economic factors to intricate decision-making processes.

3. The Role of AI in Personalized Storytelling:

Recap the exploration of AI algorithms, machine learning, and natural language processing in crafting personalized and emotionally resonant brand stories.

Outline the benefits of AI-powered storytelling, including efficiency, scalability, enhanced emotional resonance, and improved customer engagement.

4. Developing AI Algorithms:

Summarize the data-driven approach to developing AI algorithms, emphasizing the ethical and responsible use of consumer data.

Highlight the significance of understanding emotional triggers and incorporating storytelling elements for maximum impact.

5. Case Studies:

Review successful case studies of brands implementing AI-powered personalized storytelling.

Discuss lessons learned, best practices, and the impact on user satisfaction, engagement, and long-term loyalty.

6. Challenges and Ethical Considerations:

Recap the challenges and ethical considerations associated with AI-powered personalized storytelling.

Emphasize the importance of safeguarding consumer information, transparency in

121

data usage, and balancing personalization with diversity and inclusion.

7. Future Trends:

Summarize the future trends in AI-powered personalized storytelling, including advances in AI technology, predictive algorithms, and integration with emerging technologies.

Explore the evolving consumer expectations, shifting preferences, and the need for staying ahead of the curve in storytelling innovation.

8. Implementation Strategies:

Recap the steps for businesses to adopt AI-powered personalized storytelling, focusing on building a skilled AI team and integrating strategies with existing marketing approaches.

Highlight the importance of measurement, analytics, ethical considerations, scalability, and future-proofing.

Call to Action for Businesses

1. Embrace Change and Innovation:

Issue a call to action for businesses to embrace the transformative power of AI-powered personalized storytelling.

Encourage a mindset of innovation, adaptation, and a commitment to exploring new frontiers in brand communication.

2. Invest in AI Talent and Technology:

Emphasize the need for businesses to invest in AI talent, technology, and ongoing training.

Advocate for the establishment of cross-functional teams capable of seamlessly integrating AI-powered strategies into existing marketing frameworks.

3. Prioritize Ethical Practices:

Stress the importance of prioritizing ethical practices in AI-powered personalized storytelling.

Encourage businesses to establish transparent communication, safeguard user privacy, and address concerns related to algorithmic bias and data security.

4. Iterative Learning and Improvement:

Call for a commitment to iterative learning and improvement in personalized storytelling strategies.

Encourage businesses to listen to user feedback, adapt to evolving consumer behaviors, and continuously refine their AI algorithms.

Vision for the Future of Marketing and Brand Communication

1. A New Era of Connectivity:

Envision a future where AI-powered personalized storytelling creates a new era of connectivity between brands and individual consumers.

Highlight the potential for deeper, more meaningful relationships forged through narratives that resonate with personal preferences and emotions.

2. Dynamic and Agile Marketing:

Envision a marketing landscape characterized by dynamic, agile strategies that respond in real-time to shifting consumer preferences.

Discuss the role of AI in enabling businesses to stay ahead of trends, adapt quickly, and create narratives that remain relevant and impactful.

3. Inclusive and Diverse Narratives:

Envision a future where AI-powered personalized storytelling contributes to the creation of inclusive and diverse narratives.

Advocate for the representation of diverse voices, cultures, and perspectives in

125

personalized stories, fostering a sense of belonging for all consumers.

4. Empowering Consumers:

Envision a future where AI empowers consumers to actively participate in the storytelling process.

Discuss the potential for user-generated content, co-creation, and a more democratized approach to brand communication.

5. Ethical Leadership in AI:

Envision a future where businesses demonstrate ethical leadership in AI-powered storytelling.

Advocate for industry-wide standards, collaboration, and responsible AI practices that prioritize user trust and well-being.

Closing Thoughts

1. The Journey Continues:

Conclude by acknowledging that the journey of AI-powered personalized storytelling is an ongoing one.

Emphasize the continual evolution, innovation, and adaptability required to navigate the dynamic landscape of marketing and brand communication.

2. A Partnership of Technology and Humanity:

Reflect on the partnership between technology and humanity in the age of AI-powered personalized storytelling.

Emphasize the enduring importance of authenticity, empathy, and emotional connection as businesses forge deeper relationships with individual consumers.

As we close this exploration into AI-powered personalized storytelling, the potential for innovation, connection, and transformative impact is evident. The future of marketing and brand communication lies in the seamless integration of AI technologies, thoughtful storytelling, and a commitment to ethical practices that prioritize the individual

127

Other books by the author

https://www.amazon.com/author/henryeparkins